THE
MISSING DAYS

Scottish Contemporary Poets Series
Other volumes in this series include:

Gerry Cambridge, *The Shell House*
Jenni Daiches, *Mediterranean*
Valerie Gillies, *The Ringing Rock*

THE
MISSING DAYS

Kenneth C Steven

SCOTTISH CONTEMPORARY POETS SERIES

SCOTTISH CULTURAL PRESS

First published 1995
by Scottish Cultural Press
PO Box 106, Aberdeen AB9 8ZE
Tel: 01224 583777
Fax: 01224 575337

British Library Cataloguing in Publication Data
A catalogue record for this book is available from the British
Library

ISBN: 1 898218 37 4

The publisher acknowledges subsidy from the Scottish Arts
Council towards the publication of this volume

Printed and bound by
BPC-AUP Aberdeen Ltd, Aberdeen

Contents

Kenneth C Steven was born in Glasgow in 1968 but moved with his family to Highland Perthshire during his school days. He began writing early, finding the people and landscape of Northern Scotland the primary inspiration for both poetry and prose.

This book of selected poems draws on his best-known work to date, and includes pieces inspired by times in Norway, Russia and Germany, as well as many pieces from Scotland.

Two collections of his poems have already been published: *Remembering Peter* (National Poetry Foundation, 1993) and *The Pearl Fisher* (National Poetry Foundation, 1995).

Kenneth Steven has also written several novels including *Dan* (Scottish Cultural Press, 1994), which tells of the story of the last day in the life of a hill farmer as has considers the changes that have affected his life and his heritage. It is both a celebration of the beauty of the land and a warning of the threat to an ancient and precious Gaelic culture. His first children's book, *The Boy and the Blue Balloon,* was published in 1995.

Acknowledgements

The author and editor wish to acknowledge the following publications in which some of this work has appeared:

Acumen, Chapman, The Countryman, Envoi, Epoch, The Fiddlehead (Canada), Famous Reporter (Australia), Frogmore Papers, Gairfish, Gairm, Green Fuse (USA), Good Society Review, Haiku Quarterly, Iron, Imago (Australia), Life and Work, Lines Review, Moonstone, The Month, New Hope International, New Impact, New Welsh Review, The North, Northern Perspective (Australia), Oasis, Ore, Outposts Poetry Quarterly, Orbis, Poetry and Audience, Poetry Nottingham, Poetry Now, Periaktos, Planet, Poetry Wales, Pennine Platform, Poetry Australia, Quartos, Queen's Quarterly (Canada), Rustic Rub, Scots Glasnost, The Scots Magazine, The Scottish Review, Sojourners (USA), Staple, Spectrum, South, Swansea Review, Understanding, Verse, West Coast Magazine, Westerly (Australia).

Also: *Remembering Peter, National Poetry Foundation, 1993*
The Pearl Fisher, National Poetry Foundation, 1995

For Philip

HALLOWE'EN

Once upon a time our honeyed lanterns
Went in pendulums along these roads;
Faces were haunted with pondweed green
Heads steepled with wizards' hats.

All October the rivers' drums had beaten
Thick to a lashing white. Now late in autumn
The final fires died out among the trees
And bled the land to broken grey.

That night smelled of chestnuts and cold stars
Breath smoked our whispers, groups of witches
Spooked us at corners and howled our backs –
Clattered behind till our chests caught fire.

We rapped at homes along the straggled roads
Sang jaggedly our songs, remembered bits of verse
Then crumbled, broke down in mirth. Yet we left
With shiver green apples, copper hands of coins.

Now televisions murder all night long
Their luminous blue tanks light up each window
And no-one anymore will ghost these roads
For Hallowe'en.

LETTER TO NEIL IN JAPAN

Three months you have been away –
Still Scotland sees its freedom through a whisky glass
In the rosy light of New Year.

This has been the worst winter since George Orwell
Huddled in the streets of London and Paris.
An old man was found hunched over the fire
His fingers stone, his eyes frozen.

But in the corner of a south-east field
It is forever England. From there
One cannot see the blood lines cut through Yugoslavia –
The empty hunger of Russia.

Last week the Queen fell from her horse
Riding at Sandringham, broke a china wrist
The world took pictures, held its breath for news.

Nothing has changed. The empire days
Still bring sherry tears to dainty ladies
In retirement homes. Scotland will remain North Britain
Till a last winter, a blizzard that will breathe the wolves
Into our spirits again.

CLIMBER

A man, high-spanned on the sneer of a blood face
High where the eagles out-breathe
Dwindled downwards on the silken rope of a scream
Imprinted the sea.

PEARLS

At night, sometimes, a single curlew
Will cross the dark with pearls of crying.

The sound flows through the room
This dark water between sleep and morning.

A river of years with countless nights
And a pearl in every mouth.

I am a fisher with a long grasp
Opening blue mussels and keeping the dust

That has swivelled a hundred years of beauty
To the price of a single pearl.

THE LAND OF JESS AND CATH

That farm was stretched on a clay land.
Cows swung out into the fields each morning
The air lime green with summer.

In the barn I was doused with cool black light
Horses rose out of nowhere, the light a gold dust
Where straw sunbeams broke the window.

I was ten. This world had just begun.
I climbed the fat machinery and jumbled out
On tractors' backs, I learned the names of birds.

One day I too would shoulder sacks, I said,
And watch the first white shuddering of lambs
That struggled into odd-socked knees in spring.

FOX

Come upon fox cubs and they're bracken
Tumbling and rubbing in early spring
Where the sun comes down like butter
On a fat fold of the hill.

The fox is quicksand
A legend in these lost acres of hills
Hung by a brush from the shepherd's wall
Two bangs though the blind head.

WILDCAT

A lash of eyes in the sudden headlights
Of a northern road.

A ring-tailed glimpse
Escaping into shyness –
You cannot break this beast into fireside purring
Retract the claws for velvet
He is too long moorland, a heather arch
Ready for warfare.

Only sometimes
He scents the perfume of a softer tabby
Sees her Sunday sheen upon the lawns
Howls her at night.

Their kittens
Inherit the tufts of his ears, the yellow petals
Of his gaze.

THE RING

I spoke to him in Gaelic
A few words, like gold dust
Swirled from a Highland river, the last
Of an Eldorado that my grandfather
And his world possessed. It is enough
To make one gold ring about my finger
A marriage to a time that was
The last link before the rivers run dry
And the pure, good water
Stops talking for ever.

WHISPERS OF THE VOLE

I come up on tiptoe
Cowering under heather rushing with wind.

The owl will be out by now,
The turret of his head swivelling in the pine,
Moon eyes watching for movement.

At least the kestrel will have gone,
His last butterflying done in the sky –
His gimlet killings finished.

I come up like a prisoner,
Praying that clouds have pillowed the moon;
Snatch a brief quiver of food before turning,
Patter back to the darkness.

Most of my children were stabbed by birds
Swallowed without conscience.
The rest of them were eaten by the blizzards
That rock these moors all winter.

Only a few survived;
Holding their breath for every enemy,
As afraid of the world as their father.

CARSAIG

That day we drove to Carsaig
In a car pluming blue smoke. Over the edge of a hill,
And there in front of us was the whole Atlantic,
Sunlight splaying down on Jura and Colonsay,
On a harbour carved from volcanoes.

We stood there, listening,
Where the cliffs circled round like ravens
The sea folding in white crashes over a peopleless beach.

That was the day I found a dragonfly
Like a brooch of sapphires on the heather.
But nothing else, no voice or light of distant boat
Just a wasp of a little plane going into the evening
And the moon rising like a white balloon.

CHERNOBYL

In the morning it crackled across the radio.
Chernobyl, and a strange yellow light
Filled my mouth with sickness.
That day it rained,
We sludged across the moor, shining orange lamps,
The oilskins smiling water sheets,
Blurs on dead landscape, nothing
But pantaloons of mist, a few crags of deer
Battling away into nowhere. And the rain
Was heavier than ever, and I thought of Noah
And the curved bell of an ark as it came to rest
When the flood was done. But a strange yellow light
Filled my mind that day,
Filled my mouth with rain and crying –
It will not be healed again.

THE HARP

Under the burning crumble of the peat
Last spring, they found the harp.
A thousand years and more it lay
Unsung, the chords taut in buried hands
Of Celtic bards. The music curled asleep,
Its strings still resin, left full of woods
And sea and birds, like paintings in the earth,
And only curlews mourning in a bleary sky above.

They lifted out the harp, a dozen heads
All bent and captured, listening for the sounds
That might lie mute inside – the bones of hands
That once had strummed for kings. But all around
Were broken promises, the wreckage of the Viking lash
Across their history's face. The harp still played –
Remembered how to weep.

SPLINTER

Irony
Nails you, the Carpenter
To a wooden cross.

BEARS

They clamber about in brown curves
Shoulders like scaffolding, splayed-out paws
Heads that lumber about in growls.

And yet, a bear can turn dainty as a kitten
Flick a lithe slither of salmon out of black water
Or bring a paw of stickiness from the tree hive.

The cubs will roll into play with a summer butterfly
Thick as carpets, the soft eyes blink a milky brown,
Close like an infant's when the cave goes dark.

We spilled coins and beer
So they could dance in taverns –
And yet their mountains still stand uncaptured
Beyond the loss of our war.

CURLEW

As the lemon green land summers again,
Mist lies thick and breathless,
Smoking the hills, and a flint grey river
Limps out to sea. The curlews lament and keen,
All night their voices cry like girls
Whose loves are lost in war. At three
It is not dark, across the fields they pass and ghost
Their song until the dawn.
And no-one can translate that pain
Or understand the words.

VOICES

The woodpecker taps out Morse,
Crows scrawl arguing across dawn in German.

Woodpigeons make soft French love words
As little twigs of sparrows chatter in Italian.

The raven is Norse, his voice chipped from sharp cliffs
And geese squabble over Icelandic sagas.

In the middle of winter all I hear are the curlews,
Crying at night their Gaelic laments.

FLINT

On Iona there are flints. Out
Where drums of high water roll the rocks
Shining things are skipped up dancing
Grey as wolves.

I think of the caves.
Men chipped arrowtips, fine and perfect
As a wren's beak, so thin you could see the sky
Through the milky tip.

Or inland, on the broad flats of clay land
Where tractors drag up soft and black the soil,
Flint cores lie like stumps of hands, dark bronze,
Their hearts the colour of toffee.

I never brought a flame from them; sparks winked
Bright gold, the air was gunned with scent
But that was all. Only now I know
Our primitive hands have lost the skill of flint.

SATURDAYS

We used to go there for eggs –
A farm track with that green vein
Sprouting the middle rut. The farm crouched
Like some aggressive wildcat on the ground
Whose yellow eyes were windows. The whole yard strutted
And bagpiped with chickens. I always feared the dogs –
Two streamlined waterfalls of black and white,
Tongues like hot bacon, their barks
Gunning my heart with fear. But the farmer's wife
Brought us inside to the kitchen's hum,
The scent of mown hay green in the room.
We talked about foxes and new roads and prices,
My lips burned on hot tea. The eggs were still warm,
Dunged and tickled with straw.
We squeaked them in sixes into boxes,
Went out across the yard as a blue sky
Switched with swallows, waved to her wide smile
On the long bounce home.

ANNA

The river, slack in August heat
Silted grey-blue through the trees.
The sun was a hammer beating brass,
Dizzying our heads.

Our backs stooped to strawberries
Nipping the stalks, tumbling them into punnets
As the farmer bellowed along the rows
Bulling us loud to work.

But Anna was gold like wheat, shining from long summer,
Her hair ringed around her shoulders,
She laughed, told stories,
Pushed the other boys so my heart drummed.

At noon we scuffed the track, darkened the cool of the barn,
Dropped down in the hay to eat. I sat behind her,
A hundred questions in my head like circling wasps,
Yet not one ever reached my lips.

I dreamed of going barefoot to the river,
Plashing the low water, watching still
for flicks of fish that daggered through the pools,
And touching hands and swimming till the dark.

Now she's just a wild scent in my head,
A flower pressed, an imprint left on years
Gone long ago. Only when I bend each August for the
        strawberries
I touch a place called Anna in my mind.

GLEN CLOVA

I remember on five fingers
The times we visited that hotel
At the far end of autumn.

All around the moors folded away,
Smudged by rain, a few rings of lochs
Gemmed in the peat.

Fishermen thudded in each night
With the sizzle of reels, stories big as the fish
That cased the bar.

The excitement of that scent –
Tufts of pipesmoke, the red dragon of open fire,
Windows tawny every dusk with whisky light.

And in the morning, before we left,
Gold curves of butter, clouds of rolls,
And the sharp, salt stink of kippers.

ALUMBRIA

Mist at anchor in the valley bottom
Like the grey tail of a sleeping dragon.

The trees on fire across the world,
A raging blaze of amber lights.

Flint deer clicking across the bracken,
Their eyes afraid, still wise of wolves.

The water drumming from the hills like rage,
Fists tight-clenched so the bones went white.

High above an eagle bending,
A single bar of beaten copper.

Seventeen geese flagging back for winter,
Crying Icelandic, new snow in their wings.

THE LONG SILENCE

On Iona the last Gaelic speaker has died.
Last winter when the gales battled each roof and window
He was blown out and into the wind.

Once upon a time he was a tall man,
Leaning at the porch of his weaver's cottage,
His eyes like pools of the sea.

Now in the summer when the tourists come
You will hear the languages fast and loud –
But never a word of Gaelic there.

All over the western islands, the last ones are going
Like candles tonight, falling across the wind,
Their last words drowned and lost in time.

But everyone is talking, busy talking,
The radios and televisions are loud all night
And no-one is listening to the long silence.

DONALD

I see him sitting there,
His hills in the favourite window
Where lambing has come these seventy years
Easily to his hands. In the ploughed fields
That make up this face are crops of stories,
Whole ears of listening: tales of foxes,
The bad throats of ravens, strange fires
Guttering without reason on a barren moor.
He has written them across the pages of his mind
And their key still winks a little gold his eyes
Until the day he closes, and the manuscripts,
Illumined with primrose and amethyst,
Are buried in his field for ever.

FIRST TIME

The shed was thick with hay light,
Prickling breath. Feet were muffled by dung
And up in a skylight window two scissor-tailed swallows
Butterflied about in fright. The sheep were ready to lamb,
Their bellies ballooned as they lay in quiet pens
Patiently waiting. The goat saw me coming,
Turned on her chain with amber eyes like marbles
Scraped her throat in welcome or in warning.
Her back was stubborn as steel, the coat wire,
I put down my big bowl and searched for the bag of milk
Fat underneath her. But though I cursed and squeezed
Like a novice on the bagpipes, no drop came,
She only shuffled on with breakfast,
Laughing in her feed at my two farmless hands.

ABERNETHY

Just within sight of a blue wing of the Tay,
Where it silts and silvers out to sea,
A place made of pantiles, all lime and yellow
In the middle of July. We went inside
To the sudden, cool hold of the shop,
Unchanged, perhaps, since the days of soldiers,
The rationing years, the echoes of bombs on Glasgow.
The old woman's face shone like an onion,
Her knife-cuts of eyes glimmered and smiled –
This ice-cream is the last in the world, she said,
And somehow I believed her, watching the silky waves
Flow from the metal, the papers she carefully curled
To wrap them inside. I wondered if she knew
We had changed, if she'd seen the prices
Outside, in the fast world
That was turning to machines.

THE CALVINIST

The heron is a Presbyterian minister,
Standing gloomy in his long grey coat,
Looking at his own reflection in a Sabbath loch.

Every now and again, pronouncing fire and brimstone,
He snatches at an unsuspecting trout
And stands with a lump in his throat.

The congregation of midges laughs at him in Gaelic.
He only prays for them, head bent into grey rain,
As a lark sings psalms half a mile above.

HYNDLAND ROAD

The beloved west end. How often we went back,
Midnight after midnight, the amber lights shining
From the high rooms. A world between the worlds
Of purring taxis and sudden plumes of laughter,
Spring trees pink with blossom or summer windows open,
Loud with the thud of jazz. There were arguments to win,
Girls to brave and the wild madness of being free
To catch and catch again, somewhere neither young nor old,
But beautiful and far beyond price.

THE RABIES MEN

She told me how, on the coast of Ecuador,
Her father saw them in the final stages –
Their lips boiling, limbs masted to their beds
Till the last coil, the snap of the spine
Like dry wood for a fire, and that blessed end in death.
They were poor, these people, dark-tanned men
Who had come for a swivelful of gold from the rivers
To rich their children's lives, but they had fallen
Through empty streams to the stench of shanty towns,
Snatched meals over open fires, and the dogs.
The dogs were everywhere, stray things smelling meat,
A bubble of foam on their pink jaws snarling –
Bites took three days to bleed sanity away,
Then there was nothing but the sweet dream of Eden
That might have healed. These men's graves were never
        marked.
The dry rivers of their hands, the thirsty mouths
Swallowed by dust.

THE HIGH FARM

After winding the hill one stands back
Blown out. A buzzard swings,
Bending over the rush of trees. Summer
And the river browses fallow through restless fields.
At the high farm, a dog flames out the sheep,
Knots them and sinks, eyes blue as a moor loch.
There are children in gales, small dolls
On brittle strings of joy and tears.
I have five hands to guide me home, stories
Big as salmon. I hunch under the lintel
And thud the long exile from my boots.

DUNDEE

The water's oil. Out of the bladders of the sky
Low rain falls, smudging the brown tubas of tugs,
Boats skipping out on white curls of open sea.
This is Dundee. A slump on the banks of the Tay,
Left here by hammering industries, the jostle of progress.
Now unemployment's the biggest boss around.
Bored motorbikes wasp up streets, the televisions scream
Blue murder all day long. The odd lopsided seagull
Yelps Icelandic across the harbour, no fish dump
In shining waves across the piers. This place is dead.
Drive on, to the first rough edges of the north,
The fallow deer of the final hills.

JUST WAR

Far away we fight, detached divisions,
Squalls of planes with falling tumours,
Reptile tanks. But nothing here
Except long blue skies in the trees
And a simple blackbird tuning his rich throat.
The snow melting into spring again and fine horses
Burnished, turning the green fields.

We forget the fire beyond our last horizon,
Return to the growing year and gales of children
With their snowdrop laughter. We do not think
The night will sigh with bombs, burst
From our peace in twisted minds
The wreckage of its desert lives.
We have not muttered a child's cluster of words
To some God somewhere for the eyes
That go on burning in the stutter of the guns.
We close our smiles and curl asleep,
Blind in the poison gas of ageless lies:
This is just war.

ONCE BEFORE

About Christmas-time we would go there,
By the back roads, with fields of geese and a grey snow.
It was flat land, tousled in autumn with red clusters
And long stretches of poplar. The old couple
Were hewn from ash and the blown-down tree of a lost age.
They sat behind windows of blue-cold cloud,
Welcomed us with fire and tea, green rooms of holly.
And he would take goose quills in his frayed grasp,
Skill ink pens with a knife and tut his pipe.
There would be talk and a looking at old things;
The clock in the hall and the skates with their many winters,
Curled asleep in a box. Then the dark came
With frost of rough gemstones, the air pinched
With stars and balloons of breath. We had to go
That year and the year that came after,
And now I don't know the way back.

NIGHT FISHING

Autumn had sandled the trees,
Leaves shuffled underfoot, the stream
Crashed down hard through snowy bends
To smoky pools and over sudden nowheres
Drumming in quartz falls.

Then I was thirteen. I had a handline
Looped out into the water, bouncing away
Downstream. Evening was umber round our heads,
A soft owl flowed through space, sharp crystal stars
Sparked like trinkets up above.

I felt a tug, was caught
By flicks of struggle. The line muscled
Taut and strong; hand over hand I pulled
Till the silver thing leapt and gauped on the bank –
My first trout.

OTTERS

I dream of them,
Crossing like pirates the East Anglian tundra,
Ears honed to the wind, listening
For the eels that lip the tide's edge
Or some rose-bellied salmon looming upstream,
Nipping the pools for flies.

They have out-lived the yabber of dogs
That once trundled these banks to blood them.
All they fear now are the slushes of roads
That metal England, and the heavy lead
Stuffing the water with disease, turning up blind fish
And ponds to pea green slumps.

I have risen at first curlew,
Morning rolling in westwards,
To wait for them. They are made of water,
Carved out of laughter and let loose
More currents and bends in their bodies
Than a whole river.

They mean we are still alive,
That land's edges have not lost entirely
Their mapless unknown. They mean
There are still streams and the pull of fish,
A place to hide beyond our rusted losses –
Precious as freshwater pearls.

POTATO PICKING

A spun splitting of mud
The tractor goes asthmatically on, smoking,
And the baskets skud down, backs bend,
The head bloods, a blush of gold
Rushes the skirts of trees.

The tinkers are ahead,
Ingrained with tide-marks of deft generations,
Their language hot as whisky.
Eyes that sift faces, the fleet of horses
Faster than a buttoned world.

We drop to eat, raucous as crows;
The sun bends down river in oils,
Flocks of gabbling swan-water reach the falls.
We lie under sky as young, as free
As the red hawks that wink in heaven.

A POEM FOR IVARS

A picture of Latvia:
You as a boy lifting potatoes behind a horse,
Swallows ticking wings in a farmyard sky,
The generals of winter a day yet closer.

In the hungry faces, the simple hands
And this hard road through the furrows of Moscow,
I see a richer earth still living, wooden songs
That could pull your people's faith.

If a man should come now to your door
Selling motorways, a rustle of money in his eyes;
Do not buy his road, for it leads
To all our lost riches, our need of God.

FOR CALUM MACLEOD OF RAASAY

News of your dying came to me
Like a branch withered and white
Carried on distant tides,
Like the salt-whip of sea-wind that grieves the eyes.

You cut the stone of your years,
Laid an unwritten song in the road to Arnish.
Not the fine or faceted song
Of the cold demeanour of cathedrals
But the pulsing vein of a people's struggle,
The clenched furrow that is roughened by storm,
Its prow against the plough of history.

You did not carry the snarl of the bayonet
Into the cowering jabber of war
Nor was your burial bronzed by some salute of splendour;
More pure the lament over Raasay,
The peewits that wept.

RUSSIA

One hour forward in time,
And thirty years backward,
This is the land we feared,
Ploughing with horses.

Sad and beautiful tonight,
The Neva slipping to the sea,
Winter sweeping the streets and whistling
A dance tune from long ago.

Somewhere there is crying,
Long and distant,
From no-one in the night
But the land beneath.

GAELIC

It lies in pockets in the hills,
A wink of gold that has not been panned
From the older veins and the worn faces.

And sometimes on a dark river of night
I imagine it returning from the seas in its struggle
Like salmon to the birthright of the springs.

CALLANISH

I go back through the gate of the mind
Summer being stacked to dry in the long wind
And the stones crouched on the hill.

I am tired of history as ordered as streets;
The intact exhibits, their questions answered.
I have gone back to these stones.

They are circling in my mind as still as eagles
And in the solstice, a gold chain of eerie light
Flickers in fires on the peat that keeps history dark.

The moors of the memories;
Faces that still have their words about them like bracken
And the well there green, where the first men drank.

A STRANGER PLACE

Hardly the place of which carols are sung;
Just an old byre at the end of an empire
Famous for killings. That was the night
Someone crashed from the inn, roaring oaths,
Spilling a moonlight of coins. The light
Was dunged with thick warmth, straw dust
Breathed into every word. Hardly the place
To find a child born squalling in the dark;
No water, no well, no rivers of life or drink,
Just a carpenter's road going on ahead to another wood
Other nails – the beams of a stable –
Turned to the sign of a cross.

BROADFORD, SKYE

A stone's throw from the world
And a new song in dancing fiddles
Bends the streams tonight.

Talking amongst themselves
Seals gut the water,
Rub through the jagged cargo of the moonlight.

The church lies like an old wildcat,
Its yellow-lit eyes are made of glass –
It is retreating before a new tide.

And our songs are lifted from the fire tonight,
Fossils chipped from dark history,
From the eyes of our fathers.

THE WOLVES

If an ice age were to drip from the muzzle of the stars,
The wolves would come jaggedly from white pads of seas
And sniff at the dead world on its hinges.
Under long miles of silence, a frozen rush hour,
The lights falling asleep like gentle flakes,
The needles of a whining wind
Sifting through the drawers of in-blown offices and stairs
And the wires humming like raw, frost-bitten nerves.

SWEDEN IN SUMMER

Stockholm was bright as lemon trees that summer,
Poplars were the tall brushes of artists,
A fascist blue sky their paint.
Walls were gold with bees, the sea raging
With haze, boats ploughing long horns
And girls with thin skirts flirted in slow motion,
Silhouettes under the oil fire of twilight.
In the back courts, meat bled on late grills
And the moon, ripe and orange and sweet, peeled moving faces.

THE LAST DEATH

When an old woman dies in a cottage hospital
There is no-one at her bedside to print
Her last words of Gaelic in the papers,
To tell the world that her glen is gone.

But all the statesmen and all the kings
That made treaties and agreements for trade
Could never buy the shining that came from her eyes,
The peace of God when she died.

And who is to mourn her but the hills
Where the girl that she was carried water
And laughed in the loud springtide of birds
When there were songs in every window.

No roads will go back there, and the empty woods
Stand bitter at the end of time. We have lost
What her hands made, what the harp wrote –
We are poor and hungry tonight.

THE VOYAGE

A long time since I saw you, my friend
And met at eight o'clocks in red-wine light
Across the traffic from the passers-by,
Wrapped up in darkness. Talking of what had happened
Since, how little time to write the few small lines
Of lightning that had come our way. You went back
The miles of roads that led through somewhere home
Drew songs from your guitar and watched
The stars come out in high-rise flats, the night
Turn grey and whistle in the day.
And I made notes of poems on the backs of hands,
The girls I could not reach and cried
That we would cross this shallow water of our lives
To some great sea that once had sung in shells.

SUMMER

The sand of summer is in my shoes;
It came like a figure on an unsteady bicycle
Across a Dutch flatness of landscape,
A squall of gulls sown in the gentle blow of fields,
Acres of blue and sails like the kites of childhood
Dappling the forehead of the sea.

CHESTNUTS

There were always horses and mushrooms.
Autumn underfoot, stinking and red,
Hands spiked with cold and our boys' breath
Steamed like desire into blue morning.

The stick spun through cloven hooves of leaves
A green scar slashed the tree
But the chestnut with its emperor's helmet
Only swayed, the stick stubbed flat brown mud.

Over this side, further, we hissed the marksman –
The minister's house was embalmed with sleep –
And the crack came, we caught the stem,
The round fist fell, broke open treasure.

One saddle-backed circle of shining
Full as mahogany in the white-soft shell.
We stooped to worship, went home in splinters
Crying over who should keep the king.

THE WINTER BRIDGE

Dead winter. Fifteen geese
Went north in the shape of horns.

The river had stopped talking,
Clenched hard as a dead man's fist.

Bronze swords of sun battled the ridges,
Legends went by like horses in the mist.

At four the light melted into gold
And a wedding ring of moon
Slipped onto a branch of birch.

THINKING OF HORSES

Six in the morning and rocked awake
By a burning sway of sunlight. I struggled up
Thinking of horses, seeing the farm
Small-toyed below across the valley.

Alec took me there,
His wellingtons drumming along the road
Sucking the mud, as over the fields
Pibrochs of curlew trailed long laments.

The scent of horses, the memory of rides –
Rosettes poppying the stable walls,
Mahogany backs, an amber sheen
In the thick dusk of the stables.

Eyes rolling white and huge to look
The dust thumped up from thick manes
As each was clapped and given a whisper,
Slipped an unwrapped square of sugar.

KENYON

At ten he came in, dog tired
The lambing three weeks done,
Outside the sleet heavy on the fells
A big wind rocking the house.

Sixty years he's lived here
Farmer to the bone, carved out of early risings,
Wild goose chases for drowned sheep,
Drenchings when the engines flood.

Sixty years he's fought against the fox
And won no medal, just banged each blind head
To a barn door, knowing the war's not over,
Just a few redcoats less.

And I wonder how and why he keeps on in this place
Since all his work will wash away into the yard
When he is dead, and the dumb sheep blunder
Across his grave, nipping the new grass.

WINDOW

An April night, the sky not dark
But blue, green-blue, pierced with bits of stars
And a glass balloon of moonlight riding
Up from among the hills, weightless.

The house lights along the hill like pearls
The trees dead still in the windless air,
Nothing but the fluttering of an owl's call
And the deer coming to drink from the river.

HIGHLAND BULL

He is just an ornament on the moorland
Made of heather roots, too tough for meat
A piece of old machinery with handlebars
Left out to rust in all weathers.

Americans will stop their cars
In a force ten August, iron rain –
Looking for the bull's front end
And a snatched picture.

Yet in him somewhere is an engine room
Quite capable of firing.
Tickle the bracken beast
With care, with a little Gaelic.

THE CHANGING

This year the snow did not come.
All winter we waited, listening in the mornings
For that white silence, the deep blanket come back.
But nothing, just the geese scraping about the fields
Restless, unsure, and children blinking on bright afternoons
Circling their heads at the sunlight silvering westwards,
Wondering why. Christmas was warm, the soft earth easy,
Breaking beneath our feet.

It was the snow that washed away Hiroshima,
Auschwitz and Chernobyl; it was the snow
That healed our wars century after century,
Blessing us still like some strange god.

But now our winter is dying. The warm wind
Bullies the roofs, rushes demented across the world
Out of control. In its mouth autumn, spring and summer
Blown into one, as confused as the children looking
Up at the blue skies, their sledges bumping behind
Over empty grass.

And if the snow will not forgive us
What hope is there of springtime?

AGNES

That summer in St Andrews
As the sea was combing in white furls
The beach, and the wind was combing
Wild and white your hair's last curls,
I pushed you in your wheeled chair
Not knowing what to talk about
Knowing only I would not see you there again.

And you tried to remember,
You tried to pull together, like blankets and old shawls;
Names and memories and years,
And all of them just blew away like gulls
Across the sea, and when you smiled
It was a child that smiled at me.

PRAYERS

Nothing else but the robins and sparrows,
Flurrying round crumbs this New Year morning.

Above the trees a cathedral sky,
One single window of cut blue glass.

But beyond the far hill, Russia is on fire,
A dragon fighting its own tail.

Just across the river Bosnia and Serbia,
Their hands still covered with blood and dust.

Down in the valley the Marsh Arabs fighting
To keep from drowning beneath the might of Iraq.

High on these hilltops, the Tibetans crying
As China breaks them, one by one.

Under our feet, the corridors of the tortured,
The chambers in Turkey, beneath Chile and Iran.

Yet on my radio, nothing but cricket;
The state of play in another game.

Nobody seeing the blood in the rivers.
No-one hearing the prayers of their neighbours.